AGATHA

poems for the bodies in revolt

AGATHA

poems for the bodies in revolt

Lex Orgera

JackLeg Press
www.jacklegpress.org

ISBN: 978-1956907209

Library of Congress Control Number: 2023945706

Cover design by Danika Isdahl
Cover art: Sarah Goodridge. Beauty Revealed (1828). The
Metropolitan Museum of Art.

Praise for Agatha

For a long time now, I have wanted to start a convent, and now that *Agatha* is here, I can. *Agatha* will be our book of days. Our book of revelations. Our boob shop almanac. Our fallopian-dystopian book of hours. Our compendium of divine lounge chair prayer. Our atlas of bald breasts lobbed. I think these poems are what a soul assembling itself sounds like. They are ramps of energy, they are martyred and murdered efforts, they are alive and playful and full of verve and dead serious biting me with their French-tipped teeth.
—Darcie Dennigan, author of *Madame X*

Agatha orchestrates a sonorous journey through the tales we tell—and are told—of the body alive, affected, and idealized. Mythic and indomitable, the layered voices throughout parse the violence and contradictions of sainthood and monuments, living and language. "Find a saint / worth the sound of your voice," we are instructed. Orgera's is a poetics of accumulation and transmutation: breasts become couplets, syllables go missing, and euphemisms gather around a grave. *Agatha* charts a searing path into selfhood through cyclic remaking and lyric reclaiming.
—Sarah Ghazal Ali, author of *Theophanies*

Mythical and biblical, etymological and sonically exquisite, Lex Orgera's *Agatha* opens in invocation and ends in reincarnation. Journeying through states of emptiness and revolution—with "the good girl / gone wild,"—Orgera eulogizes CD Wright, riffs on PJ Harvey and Anne Carson, and pays homage to Agatha of Sicily, who became the patron saint of breast cancer patients after having her breasts torn off because she rejected her stalker. In *Agatha*'s "intergalactic orgy," wolves, ghosts, saints, dragons, and activists interact and acknowledge that even though "Dying is our common legacy," "everything shines / & primes us for shining." *Agatha* is an example of this shining: a manifesto for

survival crafted from a constellation of radiant observations and inquiries.
—Simone Muench, author of *Wolf Centos*

Enter a collection of poems that invites us to commune "where ice flower burns / orange bursts up from black needles," to stand at the edge of solemn perfection and dissolve into it. Like saints before her, Orgera's *Agatha* knows that to access the ecstatic sublime, we must regard beauty and pain in equal, material measure. In both commonplace and oracular terms, through language that, Stein-like, wakes the reader to its plentiful and even contradictory meanings, these poems allow us to relive our time here in the world until ours too becomes that more replete life of perception, until we too "ate from / the dog's bowl. Always heard // the angels / singing, always heard / them in the trees."
—Danielle Pafunda, author of *Along the Road Everyone Must Travel*

These fine lyrics thrive at the intersection of mystery and modernity, creating "a carriage of entanglements" and ever-deepening questions around collective notions of goodness, beauty, and the divine. Orgera's haunting, oracular voice emerges from a swirl of personal and saintly histories, delivering us to the mystical "green-dark" spruces bordering life's most profound beginnings and endings. This is fierce and delicate work from one of our keenest poets.
—Kiki Petrosino, author of *White Blood: A Lyric of Virginia*

Contents

Convergence

Ether

For the saints and sinners.

How I sense myself as movement. As lake or late-night radio.
As a thing that feels weighted, finds it hard to rise, break surface.
—Lars Horn, *Voice of the Fish*

Agatha is said of *agios*, which is as much to say as holy, and *theos*, that is God, that is to say the saint of God: and, as Chrysostom saith, three things make a man holy, which three were perfectly in her; that is cleanness of heart, the presence of the Holy Ghost, and plenty of good manners. Or she is said of *A*, which is to say without, and of *geos*, earth, and of *theos*, God, as a goddess without earth, that is without earthly love. Or she is said of *aga*, that is to say speaking, and of *thau*, that is perfection, that is that she was speaking and accomplishing much perfectly, and that appeareth well in her answers. Or she is said of *agath*, that is service, and *thaas*, sovereign, which is as sovereign service, and because she said that servage is sovereign noblesse. Or she is said of *aga*, that is solemn, and of *thau*, that is perfection, for the perfection was right solemn, like as it appeareth by the angels that buried her.

—*The Golden Legend* by Jacobus de Voragine, 1275; trans. William Claxton, 1483

Invocation

Sonnet from the Highest Branch

Edge, spilled milk.   Aviation is
woman's work.   So high up, we're planetary.
Edge, varied disaster.   Edge, triumvirate.
We airy birds ruled
gaily by the things inside us, not being
gods.   Indistinguishable gentry,
tinsel-grown, glory-milled creatures
over a landscape of hilled kennels
& fennel-filled & ice cream-filled,
cremated by choice.   Unferaled!
We want our ashes bare,
scattered into the dreary mouth
of a tiger.   A rarified vision, fear.
For the nest, a piece of flair.

The Lineage of Stone is a Vessel

In which sound follows the strain of lifting off.
In which why & its ancestor how.
In which you are CEO of music for the world.
In which you are a shark signifying indefinite movement rather
   than violence.
In which you play your mother on TV.
In which your lineage is not a sitcom but also not a mystery.
In which grave mistakes & gravestones are bedmates.
In which you lie in bed echo & voice, voice & echo:
         Be still, be good, be nice, be like the croissant.
In which worry is actually a doll.
In which your dress is a manifesto.
In which your mother told you
         not to wear the bikini, that it didn't flatter your belly.
         Not to walk like a man. Or dress like a man.
In which lineage.
In which she also called you her beautiful dreamer.
In which she read you poems about the sea.
         Murder burns blue on every television today.
         The binary philosophy of beating a stone for water.
In which you yield.
In which you follow.
In which self's maddening witness.
In which self is a puncture wound from a blue pen.

The Door of Your Body

Open your door, shake
out your bone-tired

arms. The door is
now, you are your-

self. Open
it, give each

limb a bath
for the sorrowful

way you have treated them.
The door is you & you

are it. Take out the hum
of childhood. The coal

in your pocket. The instance
of definition

or identity. Explain
to the door that it's just

you two in a room, that
there's nothing you wouldn't

give your door. When no one
taught you how to be

a door, you became
the door's hello &

the door's goodbye, walking
tough. Smart as a tree line.

Variations

The Pressure of the Text

from Barthes

Imagine someone tongues is no longer
language, which forms of neurosis
two edges. It all collides.
Of course, rhetoric
pleasure) unconcerned
impose upon does, for *what?*
Those doors of fools of all
conjugal sense, fires of language.
A text on pleasure occurs whenever
a miniaturization tastes for works:
future bliss,
commitments, combat are
-ity (by perversion a movement
of the head did like it (if
discourse (nothing
when it has *jelled* others,
with certain skirmishes,
the irony, which Zola's reduced to…
No "thesis," simple effect of
lovely brunette
-ysis (semiology) must.
I am interested. Else is prey.
It, the New humiliated
stereotype is of language
not given names—
realisms: the first
longer pleases anyone
unmasked, meant that he wrote
madness,
rationality); I recalled
sentences, but *someone*
outside any imaginable

must go on to the shores, proceed
(to whatever as an object of
nullity. Odd, a moment, etc.
-cal, sentiments perceive that
"moral soul")—which
present out of place, arriving.
Text means return—
if it were possible to the tongue,
not that of meaning.

Agatha's Prayer

Your words be but wind

Wonder & glory, power & sand, the way in the moonlight
over gouges in land. Unzip a skull: a painting of the process
of this thing operating: to the depths of disengagement
               men are flying. I'm a puppet.
 Clack my skull & you'll see the globe
           of a fist. Plateful of breast—

& black bone—leaving us to the wolves,
to the meat slicers in clanking armor.
Light says, wipe yourself out. No one is ready for this.
      Light out of fire, out of witch trial
               before its naming. Light the organ pipes.
After all these years of waiting,

let me be willowed & widened
on this isthmus window.

Something Like

the wind picks up & we are up
& up comes
      the wind & between
the palm fronds
                    our voices.
It's like the Pacific
after a storm,
          brown & sharks
breeching to see
daylight, to see the light
of stars muddy
with city.
      From the porch
we can't see
out & out
is where to be—isn't it? Is it out?
Out there
        the sound of a truck's
creaking, doors & people
with voices
& the wind   all around
picking up, the poets calling
the wind a horse,
        wanting
to take away & away & take,
the poets calling
on islands buffeting wind, who knew
the sound
        of dying things:
of wind & out walking
on a white beach & calling out,
I am
I said I am—

        the wind talking
like a prophet, the wind calling,
the way it confuses
                    silence
with something like sound.

Concussion Diary

i.

Fifty needles in my eye.
The front door to another question.
Basking in the bright white light
above a brackish creek, a clearing
in the pine saplings where a god lives—

I suppose I need to see what I've done
in the dark without my socks on.

Revolution

i

Coiled like a hagfish, *agathos*
is a fine paradox:

goodness, stone virtue
& slippery laughter.
If we're all descended

from some prehistoric good,
as ancient fish we are split-brained. I spell *fort* or *cellar* or *cave*
for protection—

forgetting *heart* or *pillar* or *save*.
            All my life, I've sought the miracle,
felt nostalgia for animal

instinct, a collective
body huddled against the fire. Cells remember the epicurean
delight of original sin, all that

eating & fucking & naming.
            But they've lied to us about the nature

of virtue. Agatha, saint of Sicily,
stationed herself into a tight origami rosebud
against advance. Tortured

out of her body, she died finally in the stone
arms of a prison cell.

Agatha Before the Earthquake
(Woodcut, 1488)

Silly little nipple squeezer. Woodcut geezer.
How nonchalant in my torture.

It's a bondage scene for the ages:
those tiny footprints leading away

like an invisible little ghost's. What you don't see:
I scared him off, I made a pencil out of him.

Into the fire no less! Look at the whisperers.
God: hold their tongues with two needles.

Look at the bodies piled behind.
Look at the nobles desiring me

dead. Look at my arms above the fire.
The air so clear that day & cold!

Carnivorous

I was looking in the closets
half the night, searching
in the hidden corners,
beneath piles, with my carving knife.
What small evil
could be lurking there?
A line drawn and mis-
drawn, I'm in my own home.
This is my own be-
wildered hunting.
An over-
zealous moon burnishes
twenty irises & a slice
of brick wall, outdated
peonies act out
of jealousy. What happens
in all this seeking
is carhorn blue, lazy,
the fast in fasting.
Nighttime at the up-all-night diner.
There's a haphazardry
to making order,
meaning different
landmasses to different choirs,
the hermit thrush's flute,
fractions of light pulling like time
travel through the open window,
bottlebrush trees, hope
flowers doused in gasoline.

Walking Alone, Catholic School

I think of myself walking
the perimeter

        of the playground,
first grade.

Child whose weapon is
isolation.

An alien cocoon
on the surface

of the moon, I cupped
        my own spit, licked

my busted knee, stepped lightly
over the sunning body

of the copperhead.   Baby rattle
on Mars, odd duck,

strange bird, émigré from the infinite
tree line in the sky.

        When I fell,
it was a glass

shard wedged
into my chin. Uniformed

children clustered,
pointing. To be a misfit

in the world is to be
welcomed into the Kingdom.

What but a Range
from the Sierra Nevadas

By degrees of lessness
robin stumped   foregrounded
by plantain lily   I am fewer & less
is more incrementally   finding the light-
form for the bifurcated pine   torso & two
legs   a tree in handstand   & do you
if sparks candesce   if a trail widens
do you friendly you
my sweet sound   coalesce & let what loose be
in conjunction with how many
times times five doing
slopes   banking an odd
angle as dead branches reaching
up from meadow bog   an actual number
of sanctities   my x = dictated
form   assembly
of creatures   I dreamed one young bear
ate the fur & skin from the belly
of another   a ritual of belonging
in the dream I am   belonging to me
as western sun   I carved
a sound here   where ice flower burns
orange   bursts up from black needles
hunter means huntress   push
to gathering
a tux of wilderness   an influx
to wrench form against self
the root of trail is _____
who pretends   a word means
bird hard along a sediment
of docility   I am scream   as we ascend
I hear the old man
in the mountain snoring   the man

18

from my father's forgotten
stories   the man with every answer
I dreamed as usual my father brushing
my mother's hair   into a hawk's nest
mother frowning   father emptying
cereal bowls onto the floor
father falling   avalanche rubble
to the floor   head bent   ever again
am knowing three things
am is what am knows   is all I have
all the blooming
afternoon   what but a range
of disaster sites   of leaves burnt to cluster

Concussion Diary

ii.

The snapping turtles. A farmer
        aims his gun at the sky's heart.

Wave the white flags of anaphora...
delicate moons in my plastic cup.

Like fossilized bone.
A blue blanket on the line.

Revolution

Ancient apples grow in me-
andering forest groves,

a fitting path is laid for the instigator
of the Fall, the good girl

gone wild. Bald breasts lobbed
from treetops or videos of topless lap dancing

in Key West. Is there another word
like the old English *gōd*,

meaning *good* but looking like *god*,
meant to play the act & actor both?

Upstairs from Eden, the gods
are screwing in leather office chairs,

five, six, seven glass ceilings
broken, so that they need a little

dustpan for their mess. Inside
they're cracking, they're laughter

of the highest magnitude,
insurgents searching

for groundswells of patent
energy, blankets to cover the old ways.

Alarm Clock, Easter, etc.

The motion is toward
dead mockingbirds. From the warhead
you've always walked sideways
past to hanging five-&-dime laundry
outside in a hurricane.
Nothing dies & you wonder
about slogans & tooth hooks
& who's moving the pen in your hand
or through the air, who wants
backgammon on a Saturday afternoon
to be totally ignorant
of outcomes. The garbage will
poison your brain.
The saline levels and Saturn
will destroy you.
Tsunami & volcano.
Nighttime has destructive properties.
Wake up—you begin to understand
your fissures
in chlorinated environments.
Fool's hope—*wake up*—
surrenders you.   Antarctica undilutable.
Same goes for South Carolina, South Dakota,
South Bend—*wake up*—South Orange. *Wake up.*
The memory of travel can do you in.
A cat's claw can give you fever.
A man in an alley, alone.   Half-insane
lightning, —*wake up*—unconscious song.
I've seen a snapdragon
kill a—*wake up wake up*—
your neighbor will destroy you
with her—*wake up.*   When you wake up from this,
your handwriting will change—*wake up*—

an angry crow has no problem—*wake up*—
If you don't wake up now,
the bed will wake up for you.   All the gurus searching.
Symbology for dummies.   *Wake up.*
Resurrection is an act of—*wake up*—
zombification. To wake the dead. To wake to
lips to wake to wailing to wake to wake
is all the same breathing.

Concussion Diary

iii.

Staring at the sun in the ceiling,
all stars banking to the left.

Revolution

iii

I dreamed I
wore my skin

in Technicolor, its
machinery naked

as the day
is long. Dreamed

I skinny-
dipped everywhere

there was water.
Ate from

the dog's bowl.
Always heard

the angels
singing, always heard

them in the trees.
To revolt is

to lose stride, to
jump the line, but

I only dreamed
of revolt. I was

the electrified
calm before

the oncoming
storm.

For Agatha's Body Forgotten

your promises be but rain

Or when one thinks he might
want me,

I hollow out my insides with ash
in a black pool

on the shaledust floor & he becomes
awed with what I can do—

to mine own self, true. No one wants
to touch me because I've become

a finch! A man ugly
& tepid as a clam

thought he could pitch-fork my soul,
but when he saw my act,

how stupid I could become, how dumb,
how plugged with sewer, how full

then empty of bile, I became the
church's duty, a native hen-peck—

to murder or martyr, doesn't matter—
on the rolling hills of the cross.

The Novitiate

At the back gate:
eggshells, coffee grinds,
arms on fire.

For every five people
per square acre,
a grub dies.

Just the way
life plays out.
On the kitchen table,

a pair of binoculars
as my father hallucinates
fingers in his dinner plate.

I can't live like this, he says.
I believe in the under-
carriage of his words

like a novitiate.
His language beyond language.
No more escape or decay:

collard stalks & rotting
pumpkins perched
above ground saying

hosanna into the air's
first & last freedom.
Even the compost

isn't really compost
because I can't
let it decompose.

Not Thinking but Fasting

The essence of photo-
graphic longing
as the hand makes holy
the unholy flame.
The body's an oeuvre,
potent, holy sent, nascent
on this earth, living even while
others die—the nature
of this nature, state of incantatory
being, a sweet smell
of being, a swell,
over-dwelling, letting the dream-
world soak though, waking
nervous, waking
in a wash of sweat.
Let the light shine for the dead
& dying. I'm buying dinner
this winter.
Escaping, popping,
adorning, not thinking but fasting,
the food of memory,
the instant good of nourishment
spent toward an everlasting tapping
into what we are:
ants in a jar on a fine shelf,
the zeitgeist won't have us,
you can't vilify & worship
simultaneously, a train
races by, the ink
in this pen leaks & puddles.

I was a quotient at first
divided & divided,
not thinking but fasting.

Concussion Diary

iv.

Someone dresses me
in a floral of spidery explosions.
Three shadows: one for me,
one to say, *I told you so.*

One I don't recognize,
who asks if I know her name.

Revolution

It was a long time in an unwanting
world before I met myself,
became an experiment:

irradiated heart injected
into a tiny
fish's chest for the world to watch

glowing from a tank.
Who infiltrated these guerilla ranks?

The childhood sweeping,
the jailcell darknesses?

I'm up to my elbows
in buttonwood, illegal
as the word *no.*

Scrubbing the floorboards,
heart kept in a crate
of chocolate fire ants.

Read the wooden lineation & found
displacement. To make waves
just say what's worth saying:

Here are my fingernails, kindred.
Here, my horror.
Here the dead cilia of so many stars.

Boxing Gospels: Agatha's Vision

and your menaces be as rivers that pass

Give me the scissors, said I. No service but in service to the eternal
self. No body but. In deepest lounging. These are mine!
Said I—& no one will slice them but me.
Said I—you won't have me & after
I die I'll return as soot in your thigh meat, as scabs
on your scrotum. I will eat you then.

& god said in the voice of the dispossessed:
Whip your hair into the wind.
God said, Fuck the earth. You're its mister.
God said to me, Wait! God said, Etna's my anger descending.
God said, Your babies will die in the fire.
So I had no babies.
God said, Box me & you'll win.

On Knowing

drawn from the cold hard mouth
of the world, derived from the rocky breasts
forever, flowing and drawn, and since
our knowledge is historical, flowing, and flown.
—E. Bishop

To share roots with the Sanskrit *veda*—
    nothing makes so much

sense on a bleak Sunday & the body
displaced, like physically

displaced, man nor do you know
if you are man

or you are woe-to-man, though you know—
as though in two parts in a last

life—you are whole. What sound makes
ambition, what sound violence?

I do this thing & I do it
in a denim vest, best-in-

the-tearoom. I do it best,
to see: *videre.* I do it most, to be

quickest to react to pulse
& stardom. The domain of stars,

is my point here. In the heavens,
    winners win & to be one,

to achieve one thing most.
Body is the infraction. Knowing

what one wants, a wanting, withered
plant, supplanted against doing.

Nostra Signora da Nessuna Parte

The whole drift of sky, black
& blue as a surgery. A chalk-white
egret descending

like a movie screen
into the oncoming rain.
It's less afraid of me

than I am of it—
that beak, those eyes.
Maria's shape's carved

into the funeral air, floats
beneath a silk scarf
of stars, the gold

of Angelico's halos. She once
commissioned
a painting of herself

lounging at the shore
in an olive bikini,
her hair Zsa Zsa platinum.

Her idea of eternity:
Our lady of perpetual beach bod.
Our lady of broken English,

of cash folded into palms.
Our lady of feasts, of fur coats &
grudges. Our lady of every-

where & nowhere hovering

between continents & eras—
I'm left walking in circles

mining the picture albums,
pocketing
images of my Maria—her sepia

childhood in Italy,
her last years & the pain
of a calcified silicone implant

ballooned
like a fat guardian angel
onto her shoulder—

a carriage of entanglements
like costume jewelry,
a life's razor-beaked contradictions—

empty serving platters,
designer shoes,
a string of broken rosary beads.

Posthaste

Delivered: the plum trees I'm leaving,
       I'm leaning on, leaving
in my will, a birthday full of abandons,

      the singular lowercase *i*. The *it*
of dropping off, offshoot of—
      Delivered: inhalation

of true events.   If anyone's aura might
tell truth, to tell it, to tell it
vibrate freely across soundwaves,

this is the forum. Delivered not at church
singing downriver but at recess,
in the recess of my tonsil

when the boy with the blue blue eyes
& freckles, the boy we called Birdie,
kissed my cheek once.

      Delivered:
a package from across the sea.
From a man there to my cheek.

Delivered on cue: thunder once.
Into the veil that is the wailing
      of this planet I screamed *Scam!*

but staking a precedent, nobody heard.
Say it & by god, it's so.
      The absurdity of circular

rhetoric delivered a breast on a platter.

Stubborn, box turtle head split becomes
a pair of unwaxed legs. Takes so long

to wake up from dream, deprivation
              of trumpet. With all creation
flooding. *Let it be*, sang

the Liverpool boys, all shags & levers
but what they meant was
Let it be delivered. Let the package fall.

Concussion Diary

v.

The stripe,
the herringbone,
the polyester suit,
quarrels
of dragged chairs,
slammed doors,
the gloom laid bare
from this hospital bed.
Secret cotton fibers,
cat hair, pipes
banging
in another
boneyard.

Revolution

In the midst of the fall, find a saint
worth the sound of your voice,

who wants what, according to
the weather. To let a storm incubate,

wait. If the shit hits the fan,
always blame the dog.

If it lands on the wall, read it like graffiti.

All selves dance
in the living room, a leaf outside

your window, desperate in summer's hot
bath, blathers into

manic, into ventricle, inviting
the tropical into the house

where it grows with tongues & root-
balls the size of cantaloupes.

Again, the object was *and* & wasn't
& was, as usual the object was.

Agatha at Dawn

and how well that all these things hurtle

& then we're trying
on the molecules

of sainthood, delivering
ourselves to the gods

of caffeine. We've got very little
to fight for.

Make your body mean
juggling, make it

jump from an altar.
Let them chop down

your couplets. Syllables
to rally by, fighters'

tricks or the vulcan's edge:
I was a little goat,

devil's cousin, but I let him
fall into magma.

Fornicating
grass blades witnessed.

Was a slut,
now a savior.

Once was lost. So many
dead before dying's

revelation—all papier-mâché,
delicate sword.

Convergence

What Things Become

What would it be like / to live in a library / of melted books?
—Anne Carson

A swimming pool that sings Puccini.
A country without houses.
Seventeen alphabets, new phonetics
becoming the sound of paper flapping
inside a tired air vent. A funeral dessert.
During the family meal, just after noon
the uncles calling, the aunties calling back.
A shouting of clouds, terrifying
silence of the broken grandfather
clock. Rocket engine dreams, fallacy
of the hungry rock, cracking branches
in an ice storm, treading water
amongst the trees in flood month.
In flood year, still lifes of fountain pens
& cigars, the raw scratch of claws
on hardwood. Books are like candles,
waxed puddles, Joseph's many-colored coat,
the sound of all the symphonies
playing a separate song or maybe
all the same song, each instrument
its own bit part in the cosmic dream.
My friend on the sidewalk in a navy robe.
A bath of books. Book perfume.
The smell of airplane in your suitcase
after a long flight, except the smell is book.
Old book, the tome, the anagram
& then after, your sister
becomes forest, the spruce grown
into green-dark hungry.

Then brother becomes father too
& there's a new being to swoon,
half the moon's an infant, half's a book.

Disappearance, with Coke Bottles

Heard everything disappearing.
Heard you moving
                       & I heard you
leaving—or wanting
to expand like twin coke bottles
missing
         the tiny worlds inside them.

[insert noise of grease,
a missing syllable's tin hooks, traction]

The toy piano I can't shake
                       hear it?
Beneath it the steady
undifferentiated voices—
           can't the cows hear it too?
All disappearing
                into cotton, fingers
shot up from earth. Yes!
& can't the children hear it too
in their attics.
               All disappearing things
are unspooled
         time signatures & beyond them
a treble in the forest,
               a scream
escaping sense. I'm running
through the hives
of managed bones. I'm not saying how
but the sound is of vanishing,
of there-ness
             then of emptiness.
It's an old battlefield,

buried trench coat, rusted silver star.
I'm not saying how
but it's the sound of taking
& of keeping
                of telephone wire
or bridge girding.
                    Of blood
in a wooden boat's mouth,
of whistling in a field
                    or the death
of whistling.
Earth heard itself
hearing
& I heard that too.

A Gathering

Facsimile thereof. Hyperextension.
Hero worship. Bilateral longing.
Hope for another future.
Spinal aperture. Nerve ablation.
Fixed-gear thinking. Systems analysis.
General fascination. Bird in hand.
Burning bush. Hapless road trip.
Design engineering. Folic acid.
Rendered self. Remodeled kitchen.
E-dream. Record-breaking flight.
Ocean liner. Rental home.
Compendium stream. Google search.
Vague description. Workshop sawhorse.
Heavenly sphere. Slips of paper.
Dictionary definition. Detonation
switch. Incendiary verb.
Speech pathology. Egress, ingress.
Blood vessel pathway. Heart attack.
Desire-storm. False idol.
Tweaked blueprint. Secret passage.
Glowing door in a dark hall.
Foundational knowledge.
Hope monger. Night whisperer.
Comma lover. Three crows
chasing a hawk. Stonecutter.
Cheese grater. Dinnertime.

Concussion Diary

vi.

In the childhood back yard,
a willow, the sound of falling.

A ghost whispers.

The shape of falling is a stack of books
crashing, knocked-out eye-
teeth puddling.

Someone's holding my hand,
but nobody's there.

Revolution

vi

> *hit her with a hammer / teeth smashed in /*
> *red tongue twitching / look inside her skeleton*
> —*PJ Harvey*

In my mouth was another's teeth
clinking like a cat's dried bones,

in my mouth another set
of lives, a picket fence

whose blood I feel knocking
at the walls of my new teeth,

in my mouth a satin ghost, the light-soaked
prismatic of *living the wrong life*. In my mouth

the teeth of someone who died
in a fire, who may have lived

through a fire, who said, when I die
I want my teeth to go

to charity. Which is me, which is in my mouth.
In my mouth my teeth are French-tipped.

I climb into someone else's bed
at night & feel their teeth bite my lover's elbow.

In my mouth, new skin.
In my mouth, my lover thinks it's strange

but likes it. Before those teeth
in my mouth, before all that,

with my empty mouth I would loll in bed
a porcelain comma, in my mouth

I would wonder about emptiness & chewing.
With my mouth, I'd sit in bed gumming air,

reliving infant days. Now that I have teeth
I sit up toothful. Now in my mouth

a biblical gnashing of teeth,
now a furnace casting flames, now in,

now inside, now in my mouth
my redrum twin, always asking.

Agatha's Convalescence

at the foundement of my courage

Tell me it's good to lick the wounds my animal-self mornings to
lick them clean tongue in hand I salve my chest chip the scab &
crusts from rib skin here lies woman bassinet jail cell haycast dark
explosive light of wick they did it first but I'd have mounted an
army myself I'd have sawed through lymph & fatty tissues & seen
the blood of my own christ I was going home my dress perfection
red petal halter falling avalanche of bare when he pulled it down
unfleshed me with iron I was fucking the devil knowing at once
I'd never be left alone.

Concussion Diary

interlude

These people are not real they are
not real these people are
not real they are
not real these people
are not
real they are
not real
they are
not real
they

are not real
not in my head
or out they are not
real not in my head or out
these people are not real in my
head or out of my head they are

just people of the air
the sea the sky
these people are just people
of the sea the sky just
of the sea the sky just
people of the air the sea
just people neither inside
nor outside my head just
people of the sea the sky
just here in front of us
just the people here
in front of us
who live

in
the air
the sea
the sky
here we are
again these people
are not real they are
not real they are not real
these people are not real
& they live in the sea the sky
they live in the air the sea the sky

The Kindling

When I was forty-two and seven months old, a burning light
of tremendous brightness coming from heaven poured into my
entire mind. Like a flame that does not burn but enkindles, it
enflamed my whole heart and breast, just like the sun that
warms an object with its rays...
—Hildegard of Bingen

1.

Kindle the shadow.
Enkindle the eel slinking along the shadow's bow,
light up her sister. In the time of eclipse
become one self,
or two, or three, whatever provokes
foraging on the cliffside
for borage & nettle, land
of mechanistic desire, fire an offering
to the kindling, a re-
ignition of eel & bow, of the intransigent
stalk. In a bowl balanced on the sink,
water, just water.

2.

Beneath the skyline,
a faustian pact of low-
lying moon, a pool
reflecting only sound, a cat
purring in the dark—at the edges
are where an unkindling happens, a net
untied, a skin unfastened, re-
wind the eel, rewind the shadow,
her sister, in time's bowl.
Eclipse becomes self, then.

3.

The ocean wants a mate.
Skin-sliver of white plate
against the night sings
an answer, glides
in for the landing,
asks nothing.
The sky is an anchor.

Concussion Diary

vii.

In my wings, the monks say, *shut up*.

Involuntary action: melting eyelids.
A mass of pulp, pumping blood.

The sound of my mother:
rat-tat-tat of snare drum.
My feet tossed out of bed.
Maybe I'm not alive
except in my bruised mind.

Revolution

To be good-
ness personified: the good

shepherd, the good book. Standing
at attention for the thing itself:

tied up with rope
on the prairie, becoming

a promise. In bed,
thinking *to be*

called, to have a calling—
out of a spine to grow wings,

houses & magpies because the calling
calls back. The truth of this trinity

was that we were taught how to be a *good girl*,
a meaningless, frivolous gesture,

a generational misquote.
Because we were newly formed

bone. This is how legends
are born. Green grass, the grass

on which we lay, made our ankles clack
together like winter teeth. This should have been

a sign that pleasure lives
in the body, that feathers aren't

cement, that habit grows
wings. Time knows lines

& grooves, time knows
the substance of a prayer.

Furini's Agatha

yet for that it shall not move

I'm looking back. *God*, I always look back—a recycled
Lot's wife in soft sfumato. Gazing

at my captors or my father, all manacles
& forceps & the well-smithed crab claw.

No, scorpion tail! My hair's a shackle
of snails, sin-of-torture washed, a blue shawl

eternally falling. It's dark behind:
men are mysteries, in sum. My lips parted.

As. If. Saint me, yes, but don't draw me this way—
as longing, as pink-ribbon desire, when I die.

Elegy for Carrie

Two slugs in the lettuce
began their descent just here,
they began
their purpose,
began & began, those two
slugs
as though all the universe
were a green blanket,
as though all the sky
were a porcelain
berry, as though all were,
all were amen,
amen to the slithering
thumbs soliciting warmth
from the soil,
the agelessness
of natural form like paper
on a wet floor, like tree trunks
felled in a forest, the violence
of rending,

the way she was
inserted into the news cycle—
tragically,
there is a certain density
to her leaflessness,
a pattern in the way
her branches reached,
as if in layers,
through layers,
which began as descent,
as an ending,
as though all the universe

were broken
porcelain.

Concussion Diary

viii.

I have survived the shape

of falling only to taste nickels.

A cracked pot, dying fern.

A raining monolith now, a house

of lightning now, a pickled corpse now,

the frog's auntie.

Revolution

Stop dreaming of caves
& the world dies. Tiers

of beasties tell us so, dressed
as bucktoothed angels strung

from cathedral spires. Dislodged
& ephemerated, I've watched myself,

a whole person with limbs & ears
& a cute limp, become my own stopgap

on this salt slick. I might have been
nameless, but I became

instead a city boomerang.
Every rock upheaved

became my rebellion. I'll be my own
leaving, my have-gone, my vibrato

in a sewer rat's chest, bats to pickle
my throat. Every manner of architecture

is a design dedicated to shame:
so be Gothic & transfixed & may you find

yourself, like me, aghast, pressed
beneath a city's weight.

Agatha Muses on Her Torture

I'm headed to the boob shop
to get more. Pulsating

dwarf nova wrapped in screaming
cilia & ill-gotten calcite

tongues. I'm getting a gray fist
with lashes to keep

me company. A renegade
shadow like the misplaced soul

of a wild stallion to run
through my rack. I'm buying a Bambi

to graze on my ta-tas. A duende
for my dinners. A black

seed for my melons. Oxidizing leftovers
for my cans. Thirty lead soldiers

to march through my bazooms.
A patina for my knockers.

What more could I ask for?
To die the simple death of the flat-

chested, all those euphemisms
crowing around the grave.

If Not for Their Unfixed Outlines

I follow myself to work
       from outline toward
       the inky sea,
from outline I wander
the inverse of an inverse
like an outline
       ~~at war, an armed outline.~~

Inside the outline
       pearlescent ~~monuments~~
to wilderness

& inside the outline
       most of the world's ~~oil supply~~
        puddles at the feet
of the outline
but inside the outline

& inside the outline
& then again & again
~~like entropy in a closed system~~

But outside the door
is different, a flask of
       ~~snow & outside further~~
black ocean, outside further
       midnight & the sky's outline
& stars & their outlines
       & so on
until all the words are inside
the lines where gravestones jut,
pools accumulate

how far
              the outline will run
before another outline
                  is born.

Concussion Diary

ix.

Woke at a slant,
sky a red tent, air vent, potent.

The dead are standing on pinheads.

They are my dead &
they are learning

to speak again, waltzing
on the lip of a black hole.

The galaxy next door is what, wolf?
Shoreline.

Revolution

ix

Listen beyond the lore
of morning to the chickens
& crows crowing

madder—
I hear them in the fastened hum,
the *yes*, of every-damn-breather breathing.

Fodder for the living, the dead
covet our tricks
of firing

synapse for the head's golden
repetitions—mindloop,
mindloop, mindloop.

Agatha's Last Letter

Dear Mom, it's been so long. Since back when
I followed my breath—I the Desire—
I'm dry outside to the nostril, or from it, every
which way. Lip to lip, I went mechanical, Mom,
hoisted my terrific sclerosis into a desert
outside me. I tell my mouth, *Mouth, say it dry.*
I ran a little darkness into the light, Mom.
I was so sad or afraid that you'd lost me.
I cranked up my canyon repulsion.
Me! Mono! I've donated chrome to the stop-
motion men, faded to the eastern wind.
I am the last whole sky I know.
How to drink everything before us, Mom?
Fallopian! Dystopian! The thing to eat,
it comes after the eaten thing. Love, Agatha

Concussion Diary

x.

In a stone box, my dead
whisper. A bell rings,

all the angels
are cockleshells, the birds

banging at my tree-
fort's door. I wake, I sleep.

My dead wake in the rafters.
   Wake in amber, then dusk.

All mouths
move to wonderment.

Revolution

x

Finally, eliminate
the brain-

body barrier, bury her
& birth

an unabridged
animal, sister

full of holes
& asymptotes

& god-the-mother:
everything is

quieter than before!
Today isn't like every

other day—
today is today's

revolution
around the sun.

You can't
say that about

yesterday
or tomorrow.

The Way the World Actually Ends

Petticoat, petticoat, wide-brimmed
hate. The glory of cuts.

High-heeled boots, buttoned
to the knee. Fistula, bog-

worn. Sound of pouring
blood from the wound.

Glug of honey from jar
to bowl. Honey face, sweet

cheeks. Fish lips. The frog
under a pillow. Snake in the under-

wear drawer. A car tire
on asphalt, backing down.

Running across a mountain.
Tonguing the wind while it lasts.

Howl of wolf in the abandoned
apartment building. High life.

Drowning rat in the think tank
when thinking has died.

The poet smoking
at her own funeral. The activist,

a fist. The sorest breast.
The infernal next of a never-

ending speech. Foundational
ethical rehab. Earth-

bacteria rising in the tide.
A cup of tea for the masses.

Coffee pot hurtling
through the kitchen's why.

Hibernation's rainbow.
Walking the line in the sand

as the bombs glow pink,
then orange. Intergalactic orgy.

Ether

On the Occasion of the Poet's Sudden Death

There are different kinds of dying: my heart's still not right:
all night I shake scorpions   from the Technicolor bath towel:
how do we mourn the dead   we didn't know:
truth in its austerity   smells like rank sweat:
a primal screech   in a high up tree: this is the world we live in:
sending dildos to a cowboy militia in Oregon: no our heart's not right:
we ache   for a less curated banter   on this sweetest island:
I sing Praise Be   into the heater-dry air: if I stop singing
the earth will fall into a dog's mouth   its teeth sweatered
with mawed cow parts: & black dreams
of blade grass   stamped dirt   sound of nostril breathing:
blue blue sky   all of it   all of us
a mouth opening   in the bed of ages   in the marvel bed
in the dank & fleshy sheets: we're hanging
on a galaxy's neck: nothing changes after we die
except flight   velocity   & vision of what before
we only imagined: everything shines   & primes us for shining

for CD Wright

Stopping By Pegasus for a Little Tête-à-Tête Before Swinging a Hard Left into Deep Space

In space, you can say anything,
move as slow as you want,
be as fascinated as you want. The winged horse—
its bright stars & deep-sky objects,
its quintet of galaxies,
a quasar or two—has no expectation
of bodies, having emerged
from Medusa's severed neck,
as her spirit freed from the monster
she'd become. Pegasus is content
to let a body be. Horse with a grandma's arms.
When I washed up onto the shores
of a new solar system, I was looking
for I-know-not-what, my body
having all but betrayed me on Earth,
its own systems out of orbit, out of whack,
magnetic poles on the fritz, bamboozled
by hormonal hieroglyphs. Space is the model
of slowness. I may as well be an asteroid,
hunky & screaming along. Every morning
I sit down & finesse a constellation.
No one to reprimand me.

Returned As a Piano

since I was hellbent on never being a ghost—
jetpacks chockablock with gas & oil, making pages
out of nonpages, getting healed at the boondock revival.
Like a motorcycle that won't start, I was my own
kind of activism: jawbreaker, carnival ride,
the one-two punch of the boxer, growing older.
Then the motorcycle starts & I'm spinning off soot
& sand line, cycles of salt-earth, a washing machine
tumbling through morning's light, finally the allure
of an ancient upright piano in the abandoned
living room: *Am I your twilight?* Untuned,
a piano speaks proximity & action, a bible
of resonance. When I died, I left my body as an act
of hammer or pedal. In the days of all clarity, I played.

The Last Living Dragon

…

They said flames came from my mouth.

They lay me on the couch

& flames from my mouth & the world

& all its armor went black.

How does grace hide

the body from itself? Depict me

as a saint, bar me from heaven's door.

A Note on Agatha

Agatha lived in Catania, Sicily, at the foot of Mt. Etna, from 231-251 AD. She was noble born and a "virgin martyr," according to the Catholic church. Pursued and tortured by a Roman official, Quintianus, Agatha was sent to a brothel to "overcome her resistance" when she refused his advances. There she told her captors, "…your words be but wind, your promises be but rain, and your menaces be as rivers that pass, and how well that all these things hurtle at the foundement of my courage, yet for that it shall not move."

Later, among other tortures like the rack, Agatha's breasts were torn from her body, and she was sent to prison where Quintianus forbade medical care. According to legend, an apostle of God appeared to her and healed her wounds. Quintianus next ordered her raked over hot coals naked, but during *that* ordeal an earthquake shook the city. Agatha died soon after in prison.

She was never quiet, always defiant, which enraged her tormentor.

Agatha is the patron saint of breast cancer patients, bakers, rape victims, martyrs, wet nurses, and more. She is invoked during natural disasters like earthquakes, fires, and volcanoes. During the feast of St. Agatha, it is common to find breast-shaped pastries.

She is often depicted in art carrying her breasts on a platter or holding the instruments of her own torture. Several of the Agatha poems in this collection are ekphrastic in origin.

I used two translations of Voragine's *The Golden Legend* (1275) for facts and quotes, one by William Claxton in 1483 and the other by William Granger Ryan in 1993 (Princeton University Press), but the voice of Agatha within the poems is purely my own.

Acknowledgements

I'm grateful to the editors of the following journals where various versions of some of these poems appeared:

Barrelhouse Online, "Man Builds a Guitar" ("Disappearance, with Coke Bottles") & "Something Like"
Denver Quarterly, "Sonnet from the Highest Branch"
Duende, "Agatha's Prayer" and "Agatha at Dawn"
Everyday Genius, "The Novitiate"
Estuary, sections from "Revolution"
Forklift, Ohio "Alarm Clock, Easter, etc."
Fonograf, "Multiple Choice Test" ("A Gathering")
Ghost Town, "Posthaste"
Gulf Coast, "Agatha's Letter to Her Mother" and "Agatha as the Last Living Dragon"
ILK Journal, "On Jealousy" ("On Knowing")
Jet Fuel Review, sections from "Revolution"
Memorious, "Agatha in Anonymity," "Boxing Gospels," and "Furini's Agatha"
Sixth Finch, sections from "Revolution"
SpringGun, sections from "Revolution"
SUB-LIT, "Breast Cancer is In This Year" ("Agatha Muses on Her Torture")
Vinyl, "On the Occasion of the Poet's Sudden Death"

Thank you to my friends and family in poetry and life! Always at the top of the list are Aaron and the fur creatures. I love the lot of you. Thank you to the Ol' Bard Poetry Club (Rick Bursky and Abigail Dembo) for the consistent joy of making poetry together with random words. I wrote first drafts of a few of these poems in two different groups over the years that included Shira Dentz, Aimee Harrison, Melanie Hubbard, A. McA. ("Mac") Miller, and

I'm sure others I'm forgetting. Your feedback helped make the poems better. Deepest gratitude to everyone at JackLeg Press, in particular, Simone Muench for loving and choosing this book and for the tremendous words about it; Taylor Byas for the inspired and incisive editorial touch; Erik Noonan for fielding my questions and managing timelines; and, of course, Jennifer Harris for having faith in this book enough to usher it into the world. Heartfelt thanks to Sarah Ghazal Ali, Darcie Dennigan, Danielle Pafunda, and Kiki Petrosino for your poems that light the way and for reading and describing this collection in ways that continue to slay me.

JackLeg Press Authors

jacklegpress.org

V. Joshua Adams
Mark Baumgartner
Gayle Brandeis
Scott Shibuya Brown
Michael Chin
Chloe Clark
Rivka Clifton
Brittney Corrigan
Jessica Cuello
Barbara Cully
Allison Cundiff
Curious Theatre Branch
Neil de la Flor
Genevieve DeGuzman
Suzanne Frischkorn
Victoria Garza
Reginald Gibbons
Joachim Glage
Caroline Goodwin
Brett Hanley
Summer Hart
Kathryn Kruse

Brigitte Lewis
Jenny Magnus
DK McCutchen
Jean McGarry
Rita Mookerjee
Mamie Morgan
Beau O'Reilly
Lex Orgera
Zach Powers
Karen Rigby
Jo Salas
Maureen Seaton
Kristine Snodgrass
Cornelia Spelman
Peter Stenson
Melissa Studdard
Jennifer Tseng
Gemini Wahhaj
Megan Weiler
David Welch
Cassandra Whitaker
David Wesley Williams